# Contents

# Introduction

Children are natural scientists. Their sense of wonder and curiosity about the world leads them into endless explorations and discoveries. They wade into tide pools, pick wildflowers, search for life under rocks, catch fireflies, jump in puddles, and race their shadows along the sidewalk. They love learning about their bodies and all the amazing things they can do. They notice the changing shape of the moon and clouds. They are inspired by the idea that a tiny seed can grow into a towering sunflower. And these young scientists are always bursting with questions: Why is the sky blue? Where do puddles go? Why do leaves change color?

I have found that poetry is a great way to introduce science topics to children. Students are as fascinated by words as they are by nature. They delight in the sounds of words and love to say them over and over, enjoying the way a word feels on their tongue. They are particularly drawn to poetry, with its rhythm and rhyme and musical sounds. Poetry offers a wonderful window into the natural world. Like scientists, poets observe nature with all their senses and marvel at its tiny details—the delicate beauty of a spider's web, the hush of falling snow, the salty smell of ocean air.

## Connections to the Standards

The activities in this book are designed to support you in meeting the language arts and science standards recommended for children in early childhood. See page 8, for more.

But it isn't always easy to find poems that are just right for young children. I would often look through scores of books trying to locate the perfect poems for read-alouds. It was hard to find poems that met my instructional needs and that would also appeal to my students. Sometimes the poems were too long or the vocabulary was too advanced. So I began to write my own poems to share with my students. Now I'd like to share these poems with you and your students. I hope they will lead your class to make its own exciting discoveries about language and science.

**SCHOLASTIC**

# Circle-Time Poetry
# Science

by Jodi Simpson

NEW YORK • TORONTO • LONDON • AUCKLAND • SYDNEY  **Teaching**
MEXICO CITY • NEW DELHI • HONG KONG • BUENOS AIRES  *Resources*

**To all scientists who make discoveries
each day from the wonders of nature.**

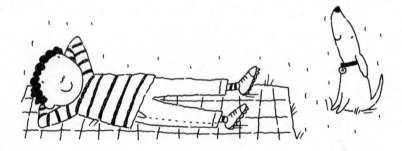

Cover art by Brenda Sexton
Cover design by Maria Lilja
Interior design by Sydney Wright
Interior art by Bari Weissman

ISBN: 0-439-52977-8
Copyright © 2005 by Jodi Simpson.
Published by Scholastic Inc.

1 2 3 4 5 6 7 8 9 10     40     13 12 11 10 09 08 07 06 05

# What's Inside

This book includes 20 poems to use as springboards for science studies as well as listening, speaking, reading, and writing activities. I like to introduce the poems to children during circle time. We continue to work with a poem during the course of a week—or even several weeks—so that children can interact with the text repeatedly. As we read a poem again and again, children become more familiar with the words and confident in reciting the lines. They begin to predict which word comes next and can focus better on the details, listening for specific sounds and searching for specific letters.

During the period of time we are working with a poem, I like to include plenty of opportunities for children to respond to it orally and in writing. We also take time to try a simple experiment, art project, or other activity that extends or reinforces a science concept addressed in the poem. To help you make the most of each poem in this book, I've organized the accompanying lessons into the following sections:

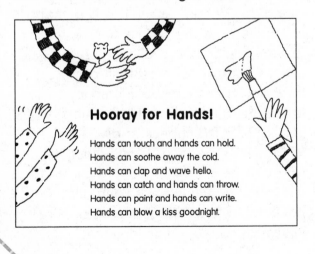

### Hooray for Hands!

Hands can touch and hands can hold.
Hands can soothe away the cold.
Hands can clap and wave hello.
Hands can catch and hands can throw.
Hands can paint and hands can write.
Hands can blow a kiss goodnight.

## Introducing the Poem

Here you'll find ideas for presenting the poem to your class. I always write the poems in large print on a sheet of chart paper. (You could also photocopy the poem pages onto an overhead.) This allows children to see clearly the words, spaces, and punctuation, and to follow along as you read. Children can come up to the chart paper and easily point out letters and words. To spark students' curiosity about the poem, I usually draw an interesting shape around it. For example, if the poem is about clouds, I'll draw the outline of a cloud around the words.

Use a pointer to track the print as you read the poem aloud several times. Children can chime in when they begin to feel comfortable with the words. You may want to invite children to act out the poem, do a finger play, or clap along to the rhythm as you read. I've included some read-aloud suggestions for each poem.

## Talking About the Poem

In this section, you'll find discussion starters to get students thinking and talking about the poem and the science topic it highlights. I want children to tap into their prior knowledge about a subject and to make connections to their own lives. I also ask specific questions about the content of the poem to check students' comprehension and ask imaginative questions to stimulate their

creative thinking. For many of the poems, I've included age-appropriate background information about a particular science concept for you to share with students.

You'll also find suggestions for getting students to interact with the text. You may wish to ask children to listen for repeated sounds or rhyming words. You can invite them to come up and point to capital letters or letters in their own names. You may want to count all the *w*'s or *l*'s in a poem, underline action words or descriptive words, point out similar spelling patterns, and so on. If you laminate the chart paper, you can use wipe-off markers to underline or circle specific letters or words. Otherwise, you can simply place self-sticking notes under the letters or words that you wish to highlight.

## Working With Words

This section includes ideas for simple games and activities to give students additional practice with some of the sounds, letters, and words featured in the poems. For example, if my students and I read a poem with several words from the *-ack* word family, I'll introduce a rhyming game to extend the learning. We may toss a ball around a circle as students come up with *-ack* rhyming words. If we read a poem that abounds with *b*'s, we might make up tongue twisters featuring the initial /b/ sound. If a poem includes words that are opposites, we might follow up by playing a game of opposites concentration. I've tried to include a variety of ideas from which you can choose and adapt according to your instructional needs and students' levels of ability.

## Shared Writing

I like to use the poems as springboards to group writing activities. Together, my students and I create simple list poems, word webs, and charts. Or we may complete sentence frames or write collaborative letters. I want children to connect with the content of a poem by sharing their own experiences, observations, and knowledge about a topic. As students dictate, I write their ideas on the chalkboard or chart paper, sounding out each letter. This is a chance to model the writing process—to show children that letters represent sounds, that words represent ideas, and that writing proceeds from top to bottom and left to right. But most important, it's a chance to give form to children's own words and thoughts. My students get a kick out of watching me write what they are saying. It's powerful to "see" language on paper, especially for young children.

## Extending the Poem

I always follow a poem with an activity that gives children some hands-on experience with a particular science theme or concept. For example, if we read a poem about fossil hunters, I like to simulate a dinosaur dig at the sand table. A poem about playing a game of sink or float leads naturally to our own experimenting with objects at the water table. A gardening activity is the natural follow-up to a poem about seeds.

## Literature Links

This section provides reading suggestions that tie in nicely with a poetry selection. I've included many nonfiction titles that offer helpful factual information about a particular science concept or theme. I've also included works of fiction to engage children's imagination.

## Reproducible Poems

Each lesson includes a reproducible copy of the poem. Students enjoy having their own copies of the poems so they can color the illustrations and take a closer look at the words. You may want to provide children with copies of the poems *after* you've introduced the poem to the entire class during read-aloud time. As you model reading for children and point out various phonological elements, you'll want all eyes focused on what you are doing. Later, when you reread the poem and continue exploring the poem's sounds, letters, and words, you can provide children with individual copies. That way students can circle and underline the letters and words on the handouts that you highlight on chart paper.

I also make a habit of sending home copies of the poems with students. It's nice for caregivers to learn the poems with children. They can then recite the poems with their child while driving in the car, setting the table, or washing the child's hair in the bathtub.

## Reproducible Patterns

Reproducible pattern pages accompany a number of the lessons. You can incorporate these patterns into the lessons in different ways. You'll find patterns for creating puppets to use as props in poetry read-alouds, for making word cards to use in sorting games and for assembling a mini science journal, among other activities. Suggestions and directions for using the patterns are included in the poetry lesson plans.

# Connections to the Early Childhood Standards:
## Language Arts & Science

## Language Arts

The activities in this book are designed to support you in meeting the following recommendations and goals for early reading and writing put forth in a joint position statement by the International Reading Association (IRA) and the National Association for the Education of Young Children (NAEYC). These goals describe a continuum for children's development in grades PreK–1.

- understands that print carries a message
- recognizes left-to-right and top-to-bottom orientation and basic concepts of print
- engages in and talks about reading and writing experiences
- uses descriptive language to explain and explore
- recognizes letters, letter-sound matches, and matches spoken words with written ones
- shows familiarity with rhyming and beginning sounds
- builds a sight word vocabulary

## Science

The activities also connect with the National Science Education Content Standards. The standards describe which science concepts students in grades K–4 should understand and skills they should develop. The list below shows how the topics in this book correlate with these standards.

### Science as Inquiry

- Scientific investigations involve asking and answering a question.
- Scientists use different kinds of investigations such as describing and classifying objects, events, and organisms.
- Simple instruments such as magnifiers provide more information than scientists obtain using only their senses.

### Physical Science

- Materials can exist in different states—solid, liquid, and gas.
- An object's motion can be described by tracing and measuring its position over time.
- The position of an object can be described by locating it relative to another object.
- Objects have many observable properties, such as size and weight, shape and color, and temperature.

- Some common substances, such as water, can be changed from one state to another by heating and cooling.
- Sound is produced by vibrating objects.
- Light travels in a straight line until it strikes an object.

### Life Science

- Organisms have basic needs—for example, animals need air, water, and food; plants require air, water, nutrients, and light.
- Organisms can only survive in environments in which their needs can be met.
- Plants and animals have different structures that serve different functions in growth and survival—for example, humans have body structures for walking, holding, seeing, and talking.
- Humans and other organisms have senses that help them detect internal and external cues.
- Plants and animals have life cycles that are different for different organisms.
- The behavior of organisms relates to the nature of their environment, including the availability of food and resources; when the environment changes, some plants and animals survive and others die or move to new locations.

### Earth & Space Science

- Earth materials include solid rocks and soil, water, and the gases of the atmosphere.
- Fossils provide evidence about animals that lived long ago.
- Weather changes from day to day and throughout the seasons.
- Weather can be described by measurable quantities such as wind direction and speed and precipitation.
- The sun and moon have properties, locations, and movements that can be observed and described.
- The moon moves across the sky on a daily basis much like the sun.
- The observable shape of the moon changes from day to day according to a monthly cycle.

### Science in Personal & Social Perspectives

- Students should engage in personal care, such as dental hygiene, to maintain and improve health.

Sources: *Learning to Read and Write: Developmentally Appropriate Practices for Young Children* © 1998 by The National Association for the Education of Young Children; *National Science Education Content Standards* published by the National Research Council (National Academy Press, 1996).

# Scientist Senses

We are scientists every day
when we read, explore, and play.
When we look closely with our eyes
at seeds and leaves and butterflies.
When we touch a stone that's smooth.
When we smell a flower's bloom.
When we hear the insects' songs.
When we taste honey on our tongues.
Yes, we are scientists every day,
making discoveries along the way.

# Scientist Senses

## Introducing the Poem

⊚ Write the poem on chart paper. Draw the outline of a magnifying glass around the words.

⊚ As you read the poem aloud, have students point to their eyes, wiggle their fingers, touch their nose, cup a hand to their ears, and point to their mouth when they hear you say the corresponding sensory word: *look, touch, smell, hear, taste.*

⊚ Invite children to try some of the sensory experiences mentioned in the poem. Provide students with magnifiers to look at seeds and leaves; use plastic spoons to give each child a small taste of honey; pass around a flower to smell and a smooth stone to touch.

## Talking About the Poem

✷ Ask children what they think scientists do. Explain that scientists make discoveries by wondering about and exploring the world around them, just as students do. Scientists observe the world with all their senses, ask questions, and try to find out the answers to those questions. What things did students notice with their senses as they got ready for school this morning? What did they taste and smell at breakfast? What did they feel as they washed up, brushed their teeth, and got dressed? What did they see and hear on the way to school? Did these sights, sounds, etc., get children wondering about anything?

✷ For fun, have students use a magnifying glass to hunt for all the initial *w*'s in the poem. How many of these words begin with the consonant digraph *wh*?

## Working With Words

**Rhyming Word Pocket Chart:** Circle the words *day, play,* and *way* in the poem. What do students notice about these words? On an index card, write the word *day.* Write the following initial consonants and consonant clusters on index cards that you have cut in half crosswise: *b, cl, gr, h, l, m, p, pl, s, w.* (Write the letters near the right hand edge of each card.) Place the letter cards along the bottom of the pocket chart. Ask, "How can we change *day* to *play*?" Invite a volunteer to place the correct letter card over the *d.* Continue challenging students to form new words by substituting letters.

## Shared Writing

**Five-Senses Science Journal:** Model sentence writing for students by writing the following frames on the chalkboard:

Today I saw a _____. Its color was_____.
Today I heard a _____. Its sound was_____.
Today I felt a _____. Its texture was_____.
Today I smelled a _____. Its scent was_____.
Today I tasted a _____. Its flavor was_____.

Ask students to help you complete each sentence. Then distribute the mini-book patterns on pages 12–14. Have students cut apart the pages, put them in order, and staple along the left side to make their own science journals. Encourage them to record in their journals words and pictures that describe sensory experiences they observe in the course of a day.

## Extending the Poem

### Popcorn Investigation

Making and eating popcorn is a great way for students to engage all of their senses.

### Materials

✳ popcorn popper     ✳ popcorn     ✳ bowl
✳ salt                ✳ napkins

❶ Give children each a few kernels of unpopped corn. Ask them to use their senses to explore the kernels. What do they look and smell like? How do they feel? How would children describe the kernels' texture? What does it sound like when they drop a kernel on their desk?

❷ Ask children to close their eyes. Make the popcorn. Can students tell what you are making by using their ears and nose?

❸ Have students open their eyes. Give each child a handful of lightly salted popcorn on a napkin. Guide children in using all their senses to explore the popcorn. How has the popcorn changed? What does it look and smell like now? How would they describe the texture of a popped corn kernel? What does it sound like as they chew the popcorn? How would they describe the taste?

❹ Emphasize to students that this is the way scientists observe the world: closely, with all their senses, noticing every tiny detail. (Safety Note: Point out to students that although they used their sense of taste in this activity—because popcorn is a food—in most cases, scientists do not taste when they work.) Encourage students to share their questions, observations, and thoughts about the activity.

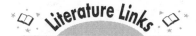

### Literature Links

These books will inspire children to explore the world with their five sensational senses:

*The Eye Book* by Dr. Seuss (Random House, 1999)

*The Listening Walk* by Paul Showers (HarperCollins, 1993)

*My Five Senses* by Aliki (HarperTrophy, 1989)

*My Five Senses* by Margaret Miller (Aladdin, 1998)

# Scientist Senses

By _____

Today I saw a _____.

Its color was _____.

*Circle-Time Poetry: Science* page 12 Scholastic Teaching Resources

Today I heard a _____.

Its sound was _____.

③

Today I felt a _____.

Its texture was _____.

④

Today I smelled a _____.

Its scent was _____.

⑤

Today I tasted a _____.

Its flavor was _____.

⑥

# Hooray for Hands!

Hands can touch and hands can hold.

Hands can soothe away the cold.

Hands can clap and wave hello.

Hands can catch and hands can throw.

Hands can paint and hands can write.

Hands can blow a kiss goodnight.

# Hooray for Hands!

## Introducing the Poem

◉ Write the poem on chart paper. Draw the outline of a hand around the words.

◉ Invite children to come up with hand gestures to accompany a reading of the poem. For example, they can hold one another's hands as you read the first line, rub their arms with their hands as you read the second line, clap and wave for the third line, and so on.

## Talking About the Poem

✳ Begin a discussion with children about all the things our hands can do. Ask: "What are some ways we use our hands at school? What are some ways we use our hands to help one another?" Extend the discussion to include other parts of the body, both inside and out.

✳ Challenge students to find and circle all the action words in this poem. Randomly pantomime these actions. Ask children to guess each word, then find it in the poem.

## Working With Words

**Initial Consonant Song:** Play this hands-on game to focus on initial *h*. Sing the following words to the tune of "If You're Happy and You Know It":

> *If happy starts with* h, *clap your hands.*
>
> *If hippo starts with* h, *clap your hands.*
>
> *Clap your hands when you hear*
>
> *the /h/ sound in your ear.*
>
> *If apple starts with* h, *clap your hands.*

As you sing, have children clap when they hear a word beginning with *h*, and refrain from clapping when they don't. Continue singing, substituting new words.

## Shared Writing

**Human Body Word Wall:** Create a class word wall focusing on the theme of the human body. Trace the outline of a child on a large sheet of craft paper. Add eyes, ears, nose, mouth, and hair. Then ask students to help you label as many external parts of the body as they can—for example, *head, neck, shoulder, chest, arm, elbow, hand, fingers, wrist, abdomen, waist, hip, thigh, leg, knee, ankle, foot, toes.* Make up simple riddles about different body parts for children to solve. For example, "I am the part of the body that can help you bend your arm. What am I?" (*elbow*)

## Extending the Poem

### Fantastic Foot Book

Students will focus on another part of their bodies in this activity: their fabulous feet.

### Materials

* old newspapers
* 9- by 12-inch sheets of white construction paper
* washable paints (various colors)
* paintbrushes
* paper towels
* several shallow pans of warm, soapy water
* black markers
* stapler

1. Spread newspapers over your work surface. Ask each student to remove a shoe and sock from one foot.

2. Have children take turns sitting in a chair as you apply the paint color of their choice to their bare foot.

3. Slide a sheet of white paper beneath each child's painted foot. The child should then put his or her foot down on the paper to make a print.

4. Help each child wash and dry his or her foot before moving on to make the next student's footprint.

5. After the paint has dried, help students write a sentence on their paper that tells something their feet can do.

6. Bind students' footprints together to create a class book titled "Feet Are Neat!"

### Literature Links

Here are some books to get children thinking about all the amazing things their bodies can do:

*Arms, Elbows, Hands, and Fingers; Body Pairs;* and *Legs, Knees, Feet, and Toes* by Lola M. Schaefer (Heinemann Library, 2003)

*Hands!* by Virginia L. Kroll (Boyds Mills Press, 1997)

*The Human Body: A First Discovery Book* by Sylvaine Perols and Gallimard Jeunesse (Scholastic, 1996)

*My Feet* and *My Hands* by Aliki (HarperTrophy, 1992)

My foot can kick a ball.

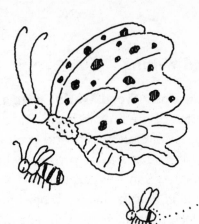

# All About Bugs

Some are red with spots of black.

Some have diamonds on their backs.

Some have stripes and some have stings.

Some have webs and some have wings.

Some can fly and some can leap.

Some can crawl and some can creep.

Some have bodies bright with light.

Some use their legs to sing goodnight.

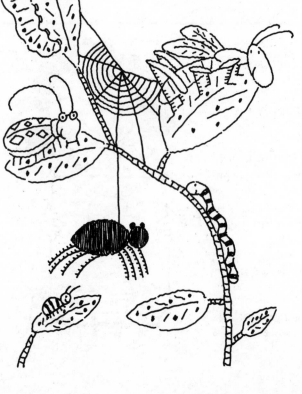

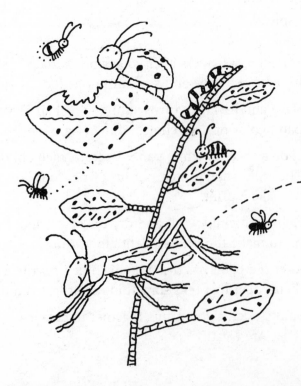

Circle-Time Poetry: Science   Scholastic Teaching Resources

# All About Bugs

## Introducing the Poem

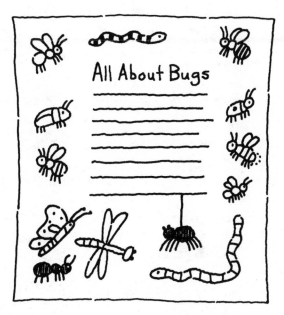

🐚 Write the poem on chart paper. Draw simple bugs buzzing, crawling, and fluttering around the poem. You may want to show a spider dropping a silky thread down from the last line of the poem.

🐚 Tell children that when we use the word *bug*, we're usually talking about insects and spiders, which are actually two different kinds of creatures. On chart paper, draw simple diagrams of an insect and a spider. (See below, right.) Explain that insects have three distinct body parts: the *head*, *abdomen*, and *thorax*. Spiders' bodies have only two parts: the head and thorax make up one part and the abdomen, the other. Also, insects have six legs while spiders have eight. Children have fun counting legs and body parts and catch on quickly about how to tell the difference between insects and spiders.

## Talking About the Poem

⭐ What kinds of bugs have students seen around their homes, at school, in the park? What did the bugs look like? What did they do?

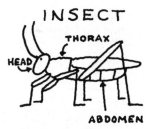

⭐ Ask students what kind of bug or bugs they think each line of the poem is talking about. For example: *Some are red with spots of black* (ladybugs); *some have diamonds on their backs* (some beetles and spiders); *some have stripes* (bees, some beetles); *some have stings* (bees). Use the patterns on pages 21–22 to make "bug buddy" finger puppets. Cut out the patterns and invite children to color them. Then fit the tabs to children's fingers using tape. Have each child wear a puppet as you reread the poem. When students hear a line or phrase that describes their "bug buddies," they should raise their puppets high.

## Working With Words

**Rhyming Beanbag Toss:** Play a simple game that focuses on some of the rhyming words in the poem. Toss a beanbag or small ball to one student. Ask, "Can you tell me a word that rhymes with *black*?" After that student provides a rhyming word, he or she throws the beanbag back to you. Continue tossing the beanbag around the circle, challenging students to come up with all the rhymes they can for the word *black*. When you've exhausted that word, choose another from the poem and continue the game.

There are so many wonderful fiction and nonfiction books available for young children to learn about insects and spiders. Here are some well-known favorites:

*Are You a Spider?* by Judy Allen (Houghton Mifflin, 2003)

*Simon & Schuster's Children's Guide to Insects and Spiders* by Jinny Johnson (Simon & Schuster, 1997)

*The Very Busy Spider* by Eric Carle (Philomel, 1985)

*The Very Quiet Cricket* by Eric Carle (Philomel, 1990)

## Shared Writing

**Buggy Sentences:** Model sentence writing for students. Begin by writing the following sentence frames on the chalkboard or chart paper, sounding out the words as you write:

Some bugs are _____.

Some bugs have _____.

Some bugs can _____.

Invite children to complete each sentence using appropriate vocabulary. Write each frame several times to give students repeated practice in forming sentences.

## Extending the Poem

### Build a Bug

Invite students to create cute clay bugs to continue their study of insect and spider characteristics.

### Materials

* nature magazines (such as *Ranger Rick, My Big Backyard,* and *Owl*)
* modeling clay or play dough in assorted colors
* colored paper
* scissors
* pipe cleaners
* shoe boxes
* toothpicks
* paint, markers, crayons

❶ If possible, cut out pictures of insects and spiders from the magazines and laminate them. Children can pass around the laminated pictures and compare and contrast the bugs' bodies. You may want to have students sort the bugs according to their physical characteristics. (If you're unable to remove and laminate the pictures, simply display and invite children to examine them.)

❷ Using the photographs as reference, invite children to create different kinds of insect and spider models out of clay or play dough. They may wish to cut out paper wings. They can also make legs and antennae using toothpicks or pipe cleaners.

❸ Let each child decorate the inside of a shoe box with art materials to create a grassy spot, colorful garden, leafy jungle, open sky, or other mini "habitat" for his or her bug to live in.

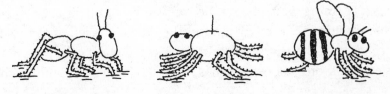

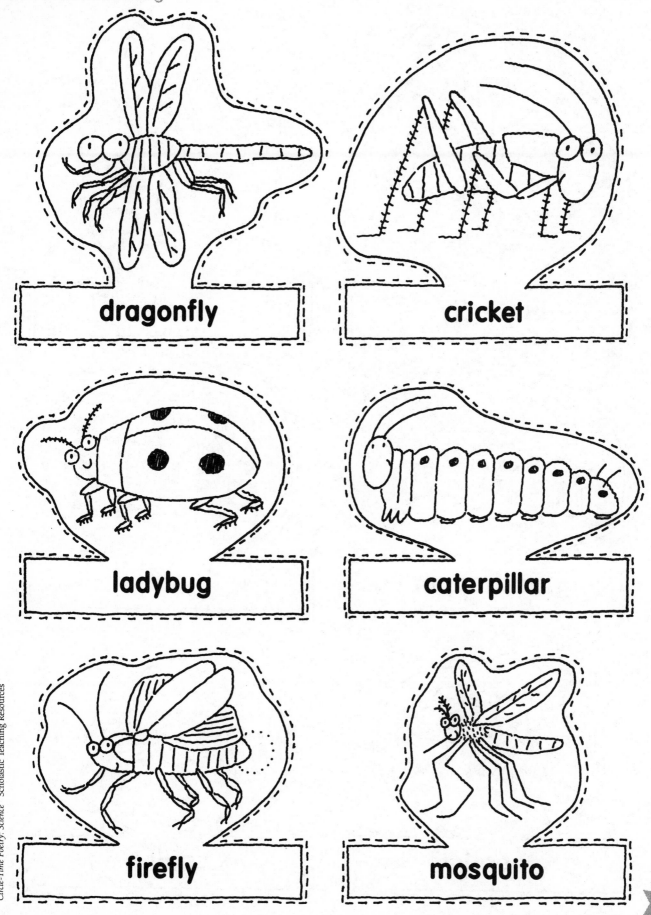

**dragonfly**

**cricket**

**ladybug**

**caterpillar**

**firefly**

**mosquito**

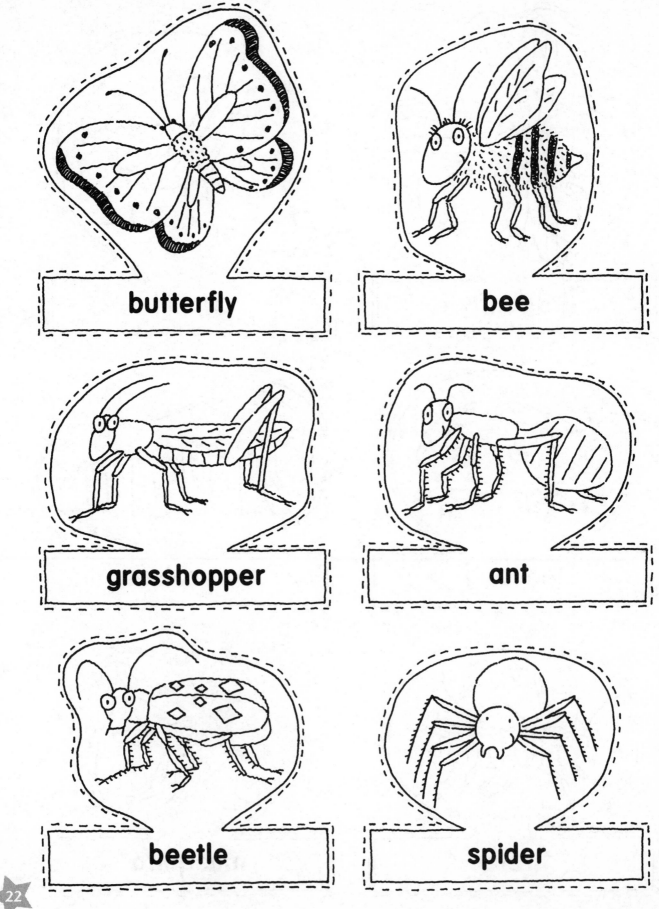

butterfly

bee

grasshopper

ant

beetle

spider

# The Dance of the Honeybee

(Sing to the tune of "Row, Row, Row Your Boat")

Dance, dance, dance around,
dance in a circle small.
Tell your hive mates that the flowers
are not far at all.

Wag, wag, wag your tail,
wag your tail to say
that the flowers are quite far
and you will point the way.

# The Dance of the Honeybee

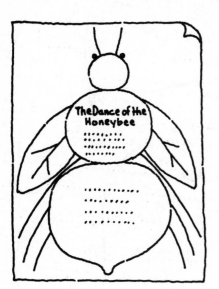

## Introducing the Poem

⊚ Write the poem on chart paper. Draw circles around the first and second stanza to represent a honeybee's body. Add a head, antennae, legs, and wings.

⊚ Before reading the poem, share some background information with students about honeybees. To make honey, bees need a sweet liquid in flowers called nectar. When one honeybee finds some flowers, it goes back to its hive and does a special dance. The dance is the bee's way of talking, or communicating. The dance tells its hive mates where the flowers are. If the bee dances in a small circle, it means the flowers are nearby. If the bee wags its tail and dances in a circle crossed by a line (similar to a wide figure 8), it's telling its hive mates that the flowers are far away. The center line points out the direction in which the other bees should fly. (See diagrams, left.)

⊚ Invite children to dance around in a circle as they sing the first stanza of the poem. For the second stanza, have children waggle their "tails" as they cross through the center of the circle in a line.

## Talking About the Poem

✸ Ask children how people communicate with one another. Encourage them to think beyond spoken words to print, hand gestures, body language, and facial expressions. Extend the discussion to include animal communication. Do students have cats or dogs? How do their pets "tell" them things?

✸ Lead children in a lighthearted, imaginative discussion about dances other animals might do to point out a food source. What kind of dance would birds do to show where worms are? What might a squirrel's acorn dance look like? Invite children to demonstrate their ideas.

## Working With Words

**Rhyming Word "Buzz":** Let children pretend to be bees as they play a game of "buzz" focusing on the *-all* word family. Explain that you are going to say a list of words rhyming with *small*. When students hear you say a word that doesn't rhyme, they should buzz like bees. For example: *small, tall, fall, ball, call, bell . . .* BZZZZZZZZ! Continue playing the game using the *-ay* word family.

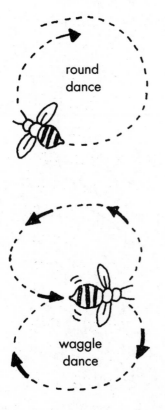

round dance

waggle dance

## Shared Writing

**Honeybee Word Wall:** Share books with students about honeybees and how they make honey (see Literature Links, right). Afterward, ask students to brainstorm a list of words related to honeybees—for example, *hive, cell, nectar, pollen, dance, communicate, flowers, queen bee,* and *worker bee.* Together, make a word wall that highlights this science vocabulary.

## Extending the Poem

### Buzzing Bee Kazoos

Students can make kazoos to buzz as they imitate the dance of the honeybee.

### Materials

- bathroom tissue tubes
- yellow tempera paint
- paintbrushes
- 5¹/2- by 1-inch strips of black construction paper
- white scrap paper
- 5-inch squares of waxed paper
- rubber bands
- pipe cleaners
- black markers
- glue sticks
- scissors

① Provide each child with a cardboard tube. Have children paint the tubes yellow.

② Give each child two black paper strips. Model how to glue the black strips around the tube to make the bee's stripes.

③ Use the hole punch to make a hole in one end of each child's tube, as shown.

④ Invite children to cut simple wing shapes from the white paper scraps and glue them to the bee's body.

⑤ Help children use the rubber band to attach the waxed paper to the end of the tube that has the hole. Children can use markers to draw the bee's face on the waxed paper.

⑥ Help children wrap a pipe cleaner around the tube to create the bee's antennae.

⑦ Demonstrate how to blow into the open end of the kazoo to make their bee buzz. Children can buzz their kazoos to the tune of "Row, Row, Row Your Boat" as they dance like honeybees in small circles and figure eights.

**Literature Links**

To find out more about how bees make honey, share these books with students:

*A Beekeeper's Year* by Sylvia A. Johnson (Little, Brown, 1994)

*Honeybees* by Deborah Heiligman (National Geographic, 2002)

*The Honey Makers* by Gail Gibbons (HarperCollins, 2000)

*The Magic School Bus Inside a Beehive* by Joanna Cole (Scholastic, 1996)

# Butterfly, Butterfly

Caterpillar, caterpillar, creep on by.
Caterpillar, caterpillar, climb up high.
Spin a cozy, warm cocoon
by the light of the full moon.
Go to sleep. Go to sleep.

Butterfly, butterfly, fly on by.
Butterfly, butterfly, fly up high.
Time to wake. Your sleep is done.
Twirl and dance beneath the sun.
Fly, be free. Fly, be free.

*Circle-Time Poetry: Science* Scholastic Teaching Resources

# Butterfly, Butterfly

## Introducing the Poem

◎ Write the poem on chart paper. Draw the outline of a butterfly around the words.

◎ Read the poem aloud and invite children to imagine they are caterpillars transforming into butterflies as they perform these actions:

**Lines 1–2:** Wiggle an index finger up your arm to your shoulder.

**Lines 3–4:** Spin one index finger around the other.

**Line 5:** Rest the side of your head on your hands.

**Lines 6–8:** Slowly stand up and spread your arms wide.

**Lines 9–10:** Whirl, twirl, and dance around.

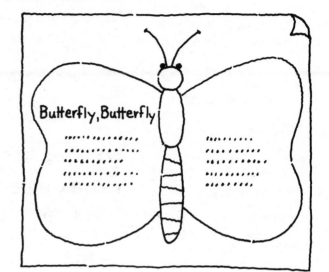

## Talking About the Poem

★ Share some background information about the life cycle of a butterfly with students. Explain that butterflies lay their eggs, which are as small as pinheads, on leaves. A tiny caterpillar hatches from an egg. It eats leaves and grows bigger. Then it hangs upside down from a twig and spins silk around its body, making a snug cocoon called a chrysalis. About 14 days later, a butterfly breaks out of the chrysalis.

★ Ask children to imagine what it might be like to be a butterfly. What would they like to do if they were butterflies? Dance in the air? Drink nectar? Sleep in the flowers? What colors would they like to be? Where would they go?

★ Have children count how many times the words *caterpillar* and *butterfly* appear in the poem. (Don't forget the title!) Can they find other words that begin with *b* and *c*?

## Working With Words

**Sleeping Caterpillar Rhyming Game:** Ask children to pretend they are sleeping caterpillars. Choose a word from the first stanza of the poem, for example, *creep*, and say a list of rhymes. When children hear you say a nonrhyming word, they should wake up from their sleep. Repeat the game, but this time ask children to pretend they are dancing butterflies. Choose a word from the second stanza, for example, *fly*, and recite a list of rhymes. Children should freeze in flight when they hear you say a nonrhyming word.

27

## Literature Links

The following books provide additional information about the life cycle of a butterfly:

*From Caterpillar to Butterfly* by Deborah Heiligman (HarperTrophy, 1996)

*I'm a Caterpillar* by Jean Marzollo (Scholastic, 1997)

*Waiting for Wings* by Lois Ehlert (Harcourt, 2001)

## Shared Writing

**Butterfly List Poem:** Create a class list poem about butterflies. Write the word *Butterflies* at the top of a sheet of chart paper. Ask children to think of words that describe butterflies— what they look like, how they move. List their ideas. At the bottom of the list, write the word *Butterflies* again to conclude the poem.

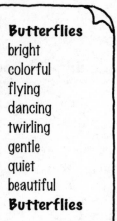

**Butterflies**
bright
colorful
flying
dancing
twirling
gentle
quiet
beautiful
**Butterflies**

## Extending the Poem

### Butterfly Life Cycle Mobile

Children can make mobiles to illustrate the caterpillar and butterfly stages in this intriguing insect's life cycle.

### Materials

* large and small paper plates          * scissors
* paints, markers, or crayons          * yarn
* hole punch

❶ Provide each child with a large and a small paper plate.

❷ On one side of the small plate, have children paint or color a caterpillar. On the other side, have them paint or color a butterfly.

❸ On one side of the large plate, have children paint or color the moon. On the other side, have them paint or color the sun.

❹ Punch a hole at both the top and the bottom of the large plates. Punch a hole at the top of the small plates only.

❺ Show children how to use the yarn to hang the small plate beneath the large plate.

❻ Tie loops of yarn through the top of the large plates and hang the mobiles around the classroom.

# We're Going to the Zoo

(Sing to the tune of "A-Hunting We Will Go")

We're going to the zoo.
We're going to the zoo,
to see some friends. I wonder who?
We're going to the zoo.

The lions will be there.
The lions will there,
with the golden manes they wear.
The lions will be there.

The elephants will be there.
The elephants will be there,
with the wrinkled skin they wear.
The elephants will be there.

The monkeys will be there.
The monkeys will be there,
with the curling tails they wear.
The monkeys will be there.

# We're Going to the Zoo

## Introducing the Poem

🌀 Write the poem on chart paper. Draw a few zoo animals around the text.

🌀 As you sing the first stanza with students, invite them to march in place and swing their arms as if they are heading off to visit the zoo. Students may enjoy pretending to be lions, monkeys, and elephants as you sing the remaining stanzas.

## Talking About the Poem

★ Has anyone in your class visited the zoo? Ask students to describe their experiences. What animals did they see? Encourage children to talk about the features that made each animal unique—the way they looked, the way they moved, the sounds they made. Which animal was their favorite? (If children have never been to the zoo, share a book about zoos with them. See Literature Links, page 31.)

★ Ask students how the poem describes lions, elephants, and monkeys. Invite them to think of other ways to describe what these animals look like. Trim sentence strips and use them to cover lines 7, 11, and 15 of the poem. Ask children to dictate alternative lines that describe each animal.

## Working With Words

**Initial Consonant Song:** To help students focus on initial consonant sounds, sing the following lyrics to the tune of "A-Hunting We Will Go":

*Lion starts with /l/. Lion starts with /l/.*
*What else can you say that starts this way?*
*Lion starts with /l/.*

Then move around the circle, asking each child to say a word beginning with the sound /l/. Repeat the game, substituting the names and initial consonant sounds of other zoo animals.

## Shared Writing

**Zoo Animal Poetry Frame:** Write the following poetry frame on the chalkboard or a sheet of chart paper:

The _____ will be there.
The _____ will be there,
with the _____ they wear.
The _____ will be there.

Ask students to help you complete the frame by naming other animals and features. Then provide each student with a copy of the poetry and picture frames on pages 32–33. (Photocopy the pages onto heavyweight paper for added durability.) Have children overlap the pages to match up the zoo scene at the top and then tape them together. Tell them to complete the poetry frame and then draw a picture of their chosen animal. Punch holes along the left edges and bind the pages together to make a class book entitled "We're Going to the Zoo."

## Extending the Poem

### A Zoo Who's Who

Students can focus more closely on animals' unique characteristics by playing this mystery animal guessing game.

### Materials

✱ nature magazines (such as *Ranger Rick*, *My Big Backyard*, and *Owl*)
✱ file folders
✱ glue
✱ scissors

❶ To prepare for the game, cut out photos of wild animals from the magazines. Choose a variety of animals with distinct physical features.

❷ Glue each picture inside a separate file folder.

❸ Close the file folder and cut out a small window on the top flap. Position the window so that it reveals a glimpse of the animal's distinctive feature— for example, a flamingo's pink feathers, a zebra's striped coat, a toucan's colorful bill.

❹ Hold the folders up one by one. Ask children to guess the animal inside based on the "sneak peek" of its physical appearance.

❺ After students have identified all the animals, cut off the top flap of each folder. Trim the bottom part of the folders as needed to make animal picture cards to use in other activities. Children can sort the picture cards according to the animals' different attributes, use the cards as reference for making up animal riddles, or shuffle and pick cards to role-play in a game of animal charades.

### ♦ Literature Links ♦

Children will enjoy meeting the zoo animals in these appealing books:

*Dear Zoo* by Rod Campbell (Simon & Schuster, 1999)

*Going to the Zoo* by Tom Paxton (HarperCollins, 1996)

*1, 2, 3, to the Zoo* by Eric Carle (Penguin Putnam, 1996)

*Polar Bear, Polar Bear, What Do You Hear?* by Eric Carle (Henry Holt, 1997)

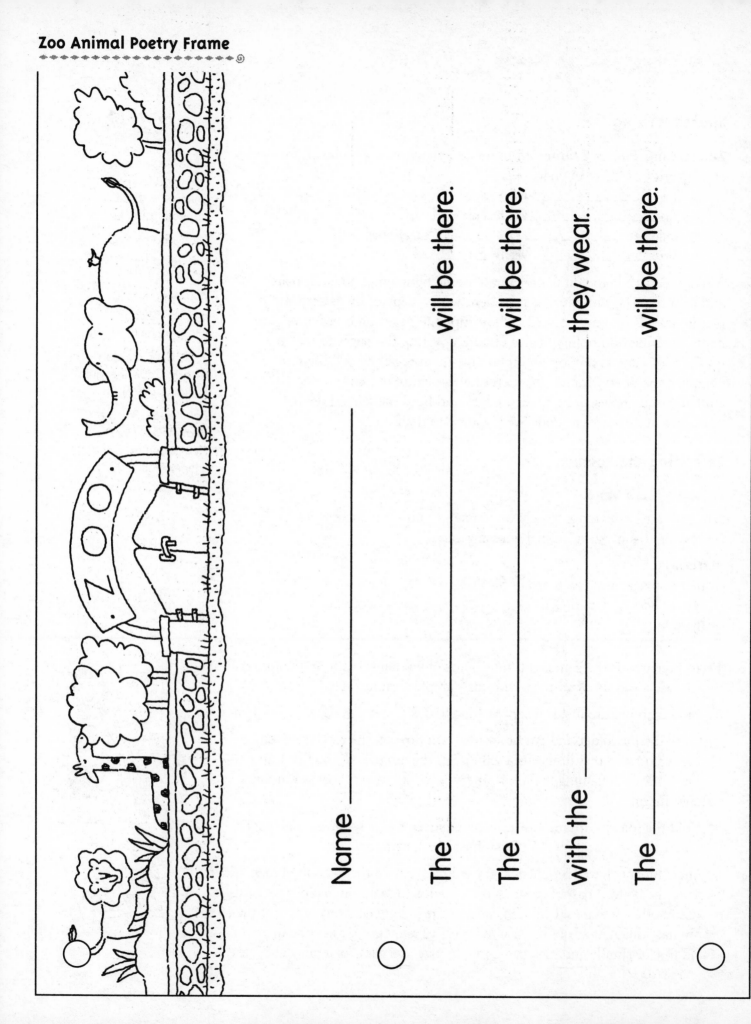

Name _____

The _____ will be there.

The _____ will be there,

with the _____ they wear.

The _____ will be there.

# Zoo Animal Poetry Frame

Cut off this strip along the dotted line. Overlap this page with page 32. Then glue or tape the pages together.

# Cozy in the Cold

(Sing to the tune of "My Darling Clementine")

We're so cozy.
We're so cozy,
even in the coldest storm.
We have blubber,
nice thick blubber,
to keep us snug
and safe and warm.

Circle-Time Poetry: Science   Scholastic Teaching Resources

# Cozy in the Cold

## Introducing the Poem

⊙ Write the poem on chart paper. Draw a large oval around the words to represent a penguin's body. Add a head, eyes, beak, feet, and wings.

⊙ Children can wrap their arms around their upper bodies to suggest they are cozy and warm, then rock from side to side as they sing the words of the poem.

## Talking About the Poem

✴ Ask students if they know what the word *blubber* means. Explain that animals that live in extremely cold places have a thick layer of fat beneath their skin. This fat, called blubber, acts like a blanket to keep their warm body heat in and the cold out. Show students pictures of penguins, polar bears, seals, and whales, all of which have blubber. You may also want to use a globe to show students the polar regions where some of these animals live.

✴ Ask students to clap out the syllables in each line of the poem to help them segment the words and hear each phoneme. Move slowly through the poem, word by word, asking students what sounds they hear. What letters make these sounds?

## Working With Words

**Initial Consonant Tongue Twisters:** *Blubber* is such a fun word for children to say. Have them repeat it several times. Ask students to count the *b*'s in this word. Then write the following silly sentence on chart paper. After students count all the *b*'s, invite them to say the sentence several times as fast as they can:

*Bobby Bear bundles in his blubber blanket.*

Challenge students to come up with additional *b* words that they can use to create new silly sentences.

## Shared Writing

**Keeping Cozy Word Web:** Ask students to think of all the ways they stay cozy in the cold. Make a web to show their ideas.

Children can travel to the Arctic by way of these books, which offer a closer look at penguins and how blubber insulates animals against the cold:

*Amazing Arctic Animals* by Jackie Glassman, (Grosset & Dunlap, 2002)

*The Emperor's Egg* by Martin Jenkins (Candlewick Press, 1999)

*The Magic School Bus in the Arctic: A Book About Heat* by Joanna Cole (Scholastic, 1998)

## Extending the Poem

### Blubber Bag Warm-Up

Students can experience the insulating effects of blubber by wearing a special "fat glove" as they submerge their hand in icy water.

### Materials

* 2 sandwich-size self-sealing plastic bags
* shortening
* measuring cup
* spoon
* tub of ice water
* paper towels

1. Scoop one cup of shortening into a bag.

2. Open the second bag and turn it inside out. Slip this bag inside the first, and then zip the edges of the two bags together.

3. Press and push around the shortening in the outer bag until it surrounds the interior bag.

4. Explain to students that shortening is a form of fat similar to blubber. Tell them that they are going to put the fat glove on one hand, then dunk both their hands in the icy water. Ask children if they think there will be any difference in how cold their two hands feel. Which hand might feel warmer? Why?

5. Have children take turns wearing the fat bag and submerging their hands. Encourage students to share their observations. Do they notice a difference in how their two hands feel? Can they keep their blubber-covered hand in the water longer? Afterward, discuss the experiment's results. Were students' guesses about the effects of the fat glove correct?

# Where Do You Go, Birds?

Where do you go, birds?

Where do you go

when the weather turns cold?

Over busy playgrounds?

Over pointed rooftops?

Over wide rivers?

Over crystal lakes?

Over quiet treetops?

Over blowing prairies?

Over tall mountains?

Over floating clouds?

Where do you go, birds?

Where do you go?

# Where Do You Go, Birds?

Where Do You Go, Birds?

## Introducing the Poem

◎ Write the poem on chart paper. Draw a V shape of migrating birds around the text.

◎ As you read the poem aloud, invite children to pretend to be birds, flapping their arms for wings.

## Talking About the Poem

★ What do students notice at the end of almost every line in the poem? Do they know what these squiggly marks are called? What is the speaker in the poem asking the birds? Are there any questions that students would like to ask birds?

★ Ask students if they know why the birds in the poem are leaving. Explain that when colder weather arrives in fall and winter, many birds fly away to warmer places. This is called migration. It may be helpful to use a map or globe to show children the colder northern regions birds leave and the warmer southern regions they fly to.

★ Do students know what the words *crystal* and *prairies* mean? Solicit their ideas before providing definitions.

★ Ask children to find all the describing words in the poem. Cover these words with sticky notes and have students provide substitutes.

## Working With Words

**Naming Word Match-Up:** Let children take turns pretending to be migrating birds as they practice identifying some of the naming words in the poem. Write the words *playgrounds, rooftops, rivers, lakes, treetops, prairies, mountains,* and *clouds* on separate index cards. Cut pictures from magazines that depict each of these things. Glue each picture to a large index card. Review the word and picture cards with students. Then place the word cards around the classroom where they are clearly visible. Place the picture cards in the center of the circle of children. Choose a child's name and say, "Where do you go, Abby?" That child should then take a card from the center of the circle and respond based on the picture— for example, "I go over the mountains." The child then "migrates" to the matching word card. Continue playing until all students have had a chance to migrate.

## Shared Writing

**Creative Questions:** What else might birds see on their journeys? Invite children to dictate new lines to add to the poem, following the same pattern.

**Where Do You Go, Birds?**

Over blue oceans?
Over sandy deserts?
Over green forests?
Over speeding cars?

## Extending the Poem

### Migrating Bird Mural

Children can collaborate on a mural featuring migrating birds fashioned from outlines of their own hands.

### Materials

- brown construction paper
- pencils
- paints, crayons, or markers
- bulletin board paper
- scissors
- glue
- black marker

**Literature Links**

The following books explain migration to young children in easy-to-understand formats:

*Honk! Honk!* by Mick Manning (Houghton Mifflin, 1997)

*How Do Birds Find Their Way?* by Roma Gans (HarperCollins, 1996)

*Lost Little Robin* by Howard Goldsmith (McGraw-Hill, 1998)

1. Divide the class into pairs, and have partners take turns tracing each other's hands onto construction paper. Students should place their hands side by side with their thumbs aligned, so that they resemble flying birds.

2. Have children cut out their birds and set them aside.

3. Roll out a large section of bulletin board paper. Provide children with the drawing materials and have them create scenery for the migrating birds to fly above. Encourage children to draw geographical features mentioned in the poem, such as playgrounds, rooftops, trees, rivers, and mountains. Students should draw the scenery on the bottom half of the paper. They can color the top half blue to resemble the sky.

4. When the scenery is finished, children can glue their birds to the top part of the bulletin board paper.

5. Use the marker to write the poem "Where Do You Go, Birds?" directly on the mural and display.

# The Seashell's Secret

"I'll tell you a secret,"
whispered the shell.
"My animal left me
alone to dwell.
So I waited for a wave
to catch a ride
and reached the beach
on a friendly tide.
Then I sat in the sand
by the water's white foam
till you came along
to carry me home."

*Circle-Time Poetry: Science*  Scholastic Teaching Resources

# The Seashell's Secret

## Introducing the Poem

◎ Write the poem on chart paper. Draw the outline of a shell around the words.

◎ Read the poem in a whispery voice, as if you are the seashell telling its story. Children can pretend they are holding shells to their ears, listening to the seashell share its secret.

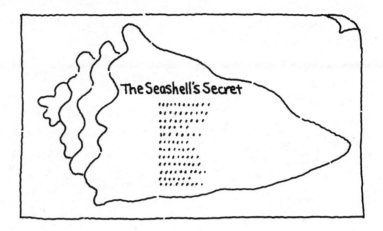

## Talking About the Poem

✸ Ask students if they have ever collected seashells on a beach. (If not, share books about sea creatures that live in shells. See Literature Links, page 42.) Explain that animals called mollusks once lived inside the shells. Clams, mussels, and oysters are all mollusks. These animals produce a material called lime to make their hard shells. During their lifetimes, mollusks add layer upon layer of lime to their shells. The shells protect mollusks' soft bodies.

✸ Take time to discuss some of the more challenging vocabulary in the poem, such as *dwell, tide,* and *foam.*

✸ Ask students what sound they hear at the beginning of the words *shell* and *shore.* Can they think of other words that begin with the /sh/ sound?

## Working With Words

**Digraph Word Sort:** Create two sets of word cards. On one set of cards, write words beginning with the /sh/ sound, such as *shell, shore, shark, ship, shoe, shout, shop,* and *share.* On the second set of cards, write words that begin with the /s/ sound, such as *sea, soap, sock, sip, sad, sick, side,* and *sack.* Shuffle the cards together and read the words one by one. Ask children to listen closely and decide whether the word begins with /sh/ or /s/. After students correctly identify the sound, show them the spelling of the word on the card. Display the cards in two separate columns on a pocket chart.

## Shared Writing

**Seashell Attribute Chart:** Pass around a variety of seashells. Allow time for children to examine the shells closely—to feel their textures and compare their shapes, sizes, and colors. You may wish to provide children with magnifying glasses. Together, create a three-column chart on which you record some of the

*(Continues)*

**Literature Links**

Explore shells and the creatures who inhabit them with these books:

*A House for a Hermit Crab* by Eric Carle (Simon & Schuster, 1991)

*Seashells* by Ann O. Squire (Scholastic, 2002)

*Seashells by the Seashore* by Marianne Collins Berkes (Dawn Publications, 2002)

*What Lives in a Shell?* by Kathleen Weidner Zoehfeld (HarperTrophy, 1994)

shells' characteristics. Follow up by inviting children to sort the shells according to different attributes.

| Color | Shape | Texture |
|-------|-------|---------|
| pink | round | rough |
| white | flat | bumpy |
| tan | curved | smooth |
| purple | pointed | hard |

## Extending the Poem

### Deep-Sea Dioramas

Children can create ocean dioramas to display some of the interesting seashells in your classroom collection.

### Materials

- ✴ shoe boxes
- ✴ paints
- ✴ paintbrushes
- ✴ construction paper
- ✴ markers
- ✴ scissors
- ✴ clean sand
- ✴ glue
- ✴ seashells
- ✴ yarn
- ✴ hole punch

❶ Provide each child with a shoe box. Have children paint ocean scenes inside the shoe boxes. They may want to paint a blue background with some green sea plants.

❷ After the paint dries, provide each child with a small amount of sand. Help children glue the sand to the bottom of their diorama so that it resembles the ocean floor.

❸ Give students a few seashells to glue onto the sandy ocean floor.

❹ Students can then draw fish and other ocean animals on construction paper and cut them out. Punch a hole at the top of each ocean animal.

❺ Cut several slits along the top of each child's diorama. (Adults only.)

❻ To suspend the creatures inside their diorama, show students how to tie one end of a piece of yarn to an ocean animal, then push the other end through a slit and tie a knot.

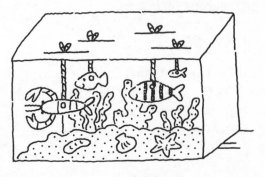

# Rain Forest, Green Forest

Rain forest, green forest,
layers of green upon green.
Rain forest, green forest,
lush leafy layers that gleam.
From the dark forest floor down low
to the canopy way up high,
deep green layers grow and grow,
brushing against blue sky.
Rain forest, green forest,
layers of green upon green.
Rain forest, green forest,
lush leafy layers that gleam.

*Circle-Time Poetry: Science*  Scholastic Teaching Resources

# Rain Forest, Green Forest

## Introducing the Poem

- Write the poem on chart paper. Surround the poem with vines and large leaves to suggest a rain forest.

- This rhythmic poem lends itself to being read chorally by two groups. One group can join you in chanting lines 1 and 2. The other group can join you in chanting lines 3 and 4. After the entire class reads lines 5 through 8, the first group can read lines 9 and 10 and the second group lines 11 and 12.

## Talking About the Poem

- Have a picture book, chart, or poster on hand to show students the different layers of the rain forest. Explain that the lowest layer is called the forest floor. Small plants that need little light grow here. Above the forest floor is the understory, which is a tangle of trees and plants that don't grow higher than about 12 feet. Above the understory is the canopy, a "roof" of soaring treetops that grow as tall as 100 feet. In the emergent layer above the canopy, trees grow even higher—up to 250 feet, which is as tall as a skyscraper. Introduce students to some of the animals that live in the forest's different layers. (See Literature Links, page 45.)

- Ask students to count all the times the word *green* appears in the poem. Then say the word slowly, stretching out each sound. What sounds do students hear at the beginning, middle, and end of the word? Can they find other words in the poem with the long-*e* sound?

- Say the phrase *lush leafy layers* in line 4 several times. Ask children what sound they hear repeated. Invite a volunteer to circle all the initial *l*'s in the poem.

- Point out the words *down* and *low* in line 5. Can children find the opposites of these words in line 6?

## Working With Words

**Opposites Match-Up:** Continue working with opposites. Write pairs of opposites on separate word cards (for example, *up/down, high/low, wet/dry, sun/rain, in/out, noisy/quiet, stop/go*). Mix up the cards and place them in a pocket chart. Challenge children to match up the pairs.

## Shared Writing

**Rain Forest Word Wall:** Ask students to think of words related to the rain forest. They may want to begin with some of the vocabulary in the poem, such as *green, layers, leafy, forest floor,* and *canopy.* List their ideas on chart paper. Provide children with simple leaf templates cut from green construction paper. Enlist children's help in copying the words onto the leaf shapes. Attach the leaves to a bulletin board to make a rain forest word wall.

## Extending the Poem

### Layers of Life on Display

Children can try this simple activity to reinforce the concept that the rain forest has four different layers.

### Materials

* 12- by 18-inch sheets of green construction paper
* markers
* scissors
* index cards
* hole punch
* yarn

❶ Have children draw large leaves on the green paper and cut them out. Each child should create two leaves.

❷ Divide the class into two groups. Then subdivide each group into four smaller groups. Assign each small group a role: a few students will be the rain forest floor, a few will be the understory, a few will be the canopy, and a few will be the emergent layer.

❸ Each child writes his or her assigned layer on an index card. Help children punch holes in the cards, loop yarn through the holes, and wear the labels around their necks.

❹ Holding leaves in their hands, students in the first large group arrange themselves to form the layers of the rain forest as the other group watches. Children who are the bottom layer of the forest should sit on the floor holding their leaves below them. Children who are the understory should kneel behind them and hold out their leaves to create branches. Children who are the canopy should stand behind the kneeling students and cover the lower layers with their leaves. Children who are the emergent layer should stand on stools or low chairs behind the other students and hold their leaves high.

# Digging for Dinosaurs

Digging for dinosaurs
in the fossil lost and found.
Searching for bones and teeth
hidden in the ground.
Dinosaur detectives
are digging in the dirt.
Sifting through the secrets
that are sleeping in the earth.

*Circle-Time Poetry: Science*  Scholastic Teaching Resources

# Digging for Dinosaurs

## Introducing the Poem

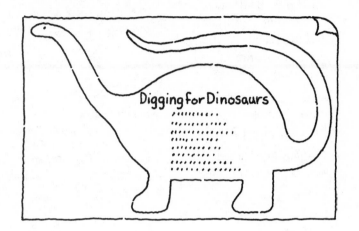

🌀 Write the poem on chart paper. Draw a simple outline of a dinosaur around the words.

🌀 Invite children to act out the poem as you read it aloud. Tell them to imagine they are "dinosaur detectives" digging in the ground. They can also hold a hand up to their eyes to pretend they are searching for bones and make believe they are sifting dirt through their hands.

## Talking About the Poem

✷ Do students know what fossils are? If possible, show them samples or pictures of fossils. Explain that fossils are the remains of animals and plants that lived long ago. Some dinosaur fossils were formed when the animals' bones, teeth, and footprints were covered with sand and mud. Over time, the mud and sand turned to rock. Scientists use shovels, picks, hammers, chisels, whisk brooms, trowels, and other tools to carefully dig the fossils from the earth. The scientists, or "dinosaur detectives," who study dinosaur fossils are called paleontologists.

✷ Underline the words in the poem that contain the vowel diphthong *ou* (*found* and *ground*). Then say them aloud, accentuating the /ou/ sound. Ask children how these words are alike. Can they think of other words that contain this sound? (Tell them that your question includes a hint!)

✷ Have children clap out the syllables in the words *dinosaur* and *detectives* to help isolate each phoneme. Ask students what sounds they hear in each syllable. What sound do these words have in common? Provide a magnifying glass and let students pretend they are detectives hunting for all the *d* words in the poem.

## Working With Words

**Initial Consonant Pass-Around:** Bring in a toy dinosaur for students to pass around the circle as they brainstorm words that begin with the letter *d*. The first child holding the dinosaur can say, "*D* is for *dinosaur*." He or she should then hand the dinosaur to the next child, who repeats the phrase "*D* is for...," substituting a new word for *dinosaur*. Keep a list of the words children come up with as they pass the toy around the circle.

## ⊡ Literature Links ⊡

For a more in-depth look at dinosaur bones and the scientists who study them, share these books with students:

*Bones, Bones, Dinosaur Bones* by Byron Barton (HarperCollins, 1990)

*Digging Up Dinosaurs* by Aliki (HarperCollins, 1988)

*Dinosaur Bones* by Aliki (HarperCollins, 1990)

*The Magic School Bus in the Time of the Dinosaurs* by Joanna Cole (Scholastic, 1994)

## Shared Writing

**Dinosaur Word Webs:** Create two separate word webs showing what students know about dinosaurs and what they would like to find out about them. Share books about these prehistoric creatures (see Literature Links, left) to help students answer some of their questions.

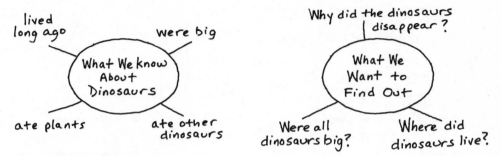

## Extending the Poem

### Classroom Dinosaur Dig

Students can pretend they are paleontologists as they excavate bones in a miniature dig.

### Materials

* chicken bones
* large pot of water
* 1/4 cup salt
* bucket
* bleach
* sandbox or sand table
* sand toys (shovels, rakes, sifters, pails)
* paintbrushes or small whisk brooms
* paper
* pencils

❶ Prepare the bones for excavation several days before your dig. Add the salt to the pot of water, and boil the chicken bones. Scrape the bones clean. Put them in a bucket, cover with bleach, and soak for two hours. Rinse the bones and set them in a sunny spot to dry for a day or two.

❷ Before children come to class, bury the bones in the sandbox or sand table.

❸ Let children use the sand toys to hunt for the bones. They can use the paintbrushes or whisk brooms to dust off their discoveries.

❹ Have children use both words and pictures to record their observations about what they found. Provide help with writing as needed.

❺ Ask students if they know what animal the bones are from. What clues from the bones support their guesses? Discuss how this activity is similar to and different from what real fossil hunters do.

# Four Seasons of Fun

Snowflakes fly in winter.
Raindrops dance in spring.
The sun shines down in summer.
In autumn, school bells ring.

In winter I wear mittens,
a coat, a scarf, a hat.
In spring I need my rain boots.
I wipe them on the mat.

In summer I go swimming.
I splish and splash around.
In autumn I can crunch my way
through leaves upon the ground.

Four seasons full of fun,
winter, spring, summer, fall.
Each one of them is special.
How I love them all!

49

# Four Seasons of Fun

### Introducing the Poem

- Write the poem on chart paper. Around the poem, draw symbols representing each season—for example, mittens, an umbrella, a sun, and a leaf.

- As you read the second and third stanzas of the poem, have children pantomime the different seasonal activities mentioned: putting on their mittens and scarves in winter, putting on their rain boots and wiping them on the mat in spring, swimming and splashing in the pool in summer, and crunching through the leaves in fall.

### Talking About the Poem

- Begin a discussion about the four seasons. What seasonal changes occur where students live? What things do students enjoy about each season? Which season is their favorite? Why?

- Use self-sticking notes to cover the names of the seasons in the first three stanzas. As you reread the poem, pause at each sticky note and ask students to name the season being described.

- Can children find the two rhyming words in each stanza of the poem? Underline each pair using a different-colored marker. Point out their similar spelling patterns.

### Working With Words

**Rhyming Word Match-Up:** Ask children to help you brainstorm more rhyming words for some of the rhyming pairs in the poem: *spring/ring, hat/mat, around/ground, fall/all.* Then write each word on a separate index card. (Make sure there is a rhyming pair for every two children in your class.) Punch a hole in the left and right corner of each card and string with yarn to make a necklace. Give each child a necklace to wear. Invite children to roam around the room, looking for a child whose word necklace rhymes with their own. When they make a match, have children read the words to each other and then sit down together.

## Shared Writing

**Seasons Comparison Chart:** Draw a four-column chart with the headings *Winter*, *Spring*, *Summer*, and *Fall*. Ask students to think of things they associate with each season, including types of weather, changes in nature, and activities they like to do. List their ideas under the appropriate heading.

| Winter | Spring | Summer | Fall |
|--------|--------|--------|------|
| colder weather | warmer weather | hot weather | weather turns chilly |
| snow and ice | new leaves on trees | school ends | birds fly south |
| bare trees | seeds grow | playing in pool | leaves turn colors |
| making snowmen | birds come back | eating popsicles | school starts |

## Extending the Poem

### Four Seasons Puppet Play

Children will enjoy making and dressing stick puppets, which they can use to act out fun activities for all four seasons.

**Materials**

* puppet pattern (page 52)
* file folders
* glue
* scissors
* fabric scraps (various colors and patterns)
* buttons
* yarn
* craft sticks
* 12- by 18-inch sheets of white construction paper
* crayons or markers

❶ Provide each child with a copy of the puppet pattern. Have children glue the pattern to a file folder and cut it out.

❷ Ask each child to pick a season of the year. Tell students to "dress" their puppets in clothing that's appropriate for this season. Children can cut clothes from the fabric scraps, then glue them on their puppets.

❸ Have children add faces and hair to their puppets, using the buttons, yarn, and crayons or markers. Then have them glue the craft sticks to the backs of their puppets.

❹ On the white construction paper, students can draw a scene in nature to illustrate their chosen season.

❺ Divide each group of children who have selected the same season into smaller groups of two or three. Let groups take turns using the puppets to act out what they might do for fun in their chosen season. Have children in each group line up their seasonal drawings along a chalkboard ledge to use as background scenery for their dramatic play.

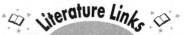

**Literature Links**

The following books are rich in visual imagery associated with the four seasons:

*Seasons* by David Stewart (Scholastic, 2002)

*Whatever the Weather* by Karen Wallace (DK Publishing, 1999)

*The Year at Maple Hill Farm* by Alice Provensen (Simon & Schuster, 2001)

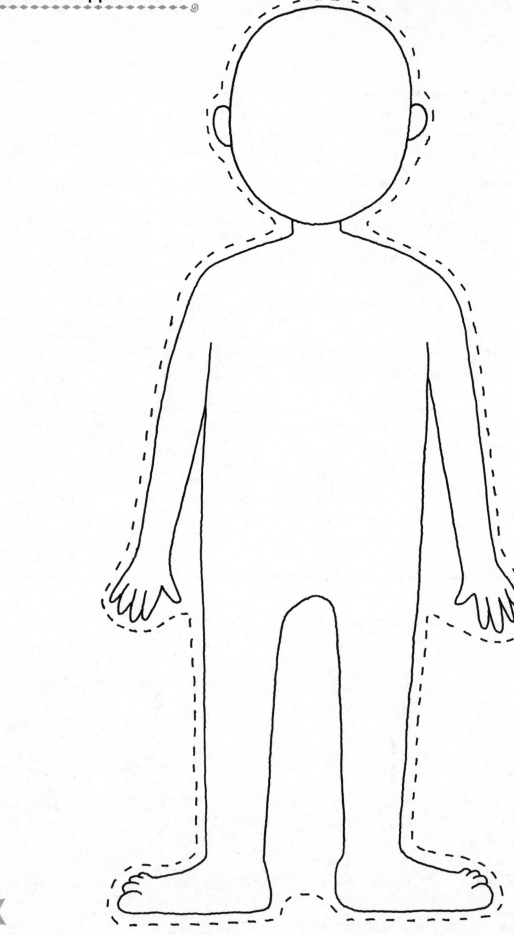

# Who Sees the Wind?

Do the trees see the wind
as it makes them sway?
Do the leaves see the wind
as it blows them away?
Do clouds see the wind
as it pushes them along?
Do chimes see the wind
as it plays their song?
Do kites see the wind
as they dance in the sky?
Does anyone see
the wind pass by?

# Who Sees the Wind?

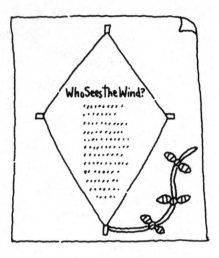

## Introducing the Poem

- Write the poem on chart paper. Draw the outline of a kite around the words.

- As you read the poem, ask children to pretend they are leaves, kites, trees, or other things being blown by the wind. Students can whirl, dance, and sway to the rhythm of the words.

## Talking About the Poem

- Explain to children that wind is moving air. Have them hold a sheet of paper in front of their mouth and blow. What happens? Can they see the mini wind they made by blowing air? No, but they can see what the wind does: It moves the paper.

- Begin a discussion about all the things the wind can do. Have children seen the wind blow a kite, flag, leaves, or sailboat? Have they felt it blow their own clothing or hair? What did it feel like? What words describe the wind? Discuss how the wind can be both strong and gentle, loud and quiet, cold and warm.

- What do students notice about each line of the poem? Point out the question mark at the end of each line. Can students tell you what this symbol means?

- Ask what sound the word *wind* begins with. What letter makes this sound? Have children count all the times *wind* appears in the poem.

## Working With Words

**Initial Consonant Blow-Away:** Make word cards for the following words: *pig, bag, cake, ball, day, bell, pet, hide, tell,* and *fish.* Snip off the initial consonants to create letter cards. Create another letter card for the letter *w.* One by one, show children the words. Hold the onset in your right hand and the rime in your left. Pronounce each phoneme. Ask children to blend the sounds together to say the word. Then ask them to pretend to be the wind blowing away the initial consonant. As children blow, remove the initial consonant letter card and replace it with the *w* letter card. Pronounce each phoneme again and have children blend the sounds together to say the new word. Children can continue to blow away initial consonants for the remaining words and replace them with the /w/ sound.

## Shared Writing

**Wind-at-Work Sentences:** Ask students to think about some of the ways we "see" the wind. How can we tell that the wind is blowing? Write the following sentence frame on the chalkboard five or six times, and ask children to help you complete it by filling in the blank.

When the wind blows, it moves _____.

## Extending the Poem

### Whirling Wind Dancers

Students can create colorful wind dancers to help them "see" the wind blow.

### Materials

* large paper plates (made from lightweight paper, not reinforced)
* pencil
* art materials (crayons, markers, paints, glitter, stickers, and so on)
* scissors
* hole punch
* yarn

❶ Draw a spiral pattern on each paper plate. Give a plate to each child.

❷ Have children color and decorate both sides of their plate.

❸ Help students cut along the lines on the plate to create a dangling spiral.

❹ Punch a hole at the top of each spiral. Help children tie a loop of yarn through the hole.

❺ On the next windy day, hang the spirals outside in a place where they can be viewed from your classroom window, if possible. Or if the weather is warm enough, hang the spirals in open classroom windows. Children can watch the spirals dance and whirl in the wind. Can they tell how hard the wind is blowing by watching the spirals move? Can they tell from which direction the wind is blowing?

**Literature Links**

Where does the wind come from and where does it blow? Share these books with children to help them find out:

*I Face the Wind* by Vicki Cobb (HarperCollins, 2003)

*Where Does the Wind Blow?* by Cindy Rink (Dawn Publications, 2004)

*Wind* by Marion Dane Bauer (Simon & Schuster, 2003)

*The Wind Blew* by Pat Hutchins (Simon & Schuster, 1993)

# Cloud Watching

Clouds, they come, they gather, they rest.
Upon the hillside, they make a nest.
Together they cuddle and huddle to form
a soft, thick quilt, so cozy and warm.
The more I look, the more clouds change
from rabbits to birds, then into rain.
Clouds, they flow, they rise, they go.
And in their place, they leave a rainbow.

Circle-Time Poetry: Science  Scholastic Teaching Resources

# Cloud Watching

## Introducing the Poem

◎ Write the poem on chart paper. Draw the outline of a cloud around the words.

◎ Invite children to lie on their backs and close their eyes. Ask children to pretend they are looking at a cloud-filled sky as you read the poem aloud in a gentle, dreamy voice.

## Talking About the Poem

✳ Ask children what pictures the words in the poem made them see. Have children identify all the things the poem says clouds look like.

✳ What do students think clouds are? Explain that clouds are made up of millions of tiny water droplets. When these droplets become big and heavy enough, they fall as rain. The sun heats the water that falls on the ground and into oceans, lakes, and rivers. It turns the water into an invisible gas called water vapor. The water vapor rises into the sky to form new clouds. This is called the water cycle.

✳ Underline the words *rest* and *nest* at the end of lines 1 and 2, respectively. What do students notice about the spelling pattern in these words? Which letters are the same? Which are different?

## Working With Words

**Floating-Cloud Word Family Game:** Cut out the cloud-shaped word cards on pages 59–60. Glue craft sticks to the back of each cloud shape. Randomly distribute the clouds to children. Ask the child who is holding the word card *rest* to pretend he or she is a cloud and "float" to the front of the class. Call out the name of another child who is holding a cloud. Have him or her float over to the first child. Ask the class to decide whether the two words on the cloud shapes rhyme. If they do, the clouds should stay gathered together. If they do not, the second cloud should float past the first cloud and return to his or her seat in the circle. Continue playing the game until all the clouds with rhyming words are gathered together. Repeat the game so that all children get a chance to be clouds.

These books show clouds' many different appearances, using both realistic and imaginative images:

*The Cloud Book* by Tomie dePaola (Holiday House, 1984)

*Cloud Dance* by Thomas Locker (Harcourt, 2000)

*It Looked Like Spilt Milk* by Charles G. Shaw (HarperCollins, 1988)

## Shared Writing

**Cloud List Poem:** Create a class list poem about clouds. Write the word *Clouds* at the top of a sheet of chart paper. Ask children to think of words that describe clouds—what they look like, the shapes they take, the way they move. List their ideas. At the bottom of the list, write the word *Clouds* again to conclude the poem.

## Extending the Poem

### Shaving Cream Clouds

For a hands-on approach to cloud watching, have children make cloud shapes using shaving cream.

### Materials

* 12- by 18-inch sheets of light blue construction paper
* laminating machine
* science journals
* pencils
* shaving cream
* paper towels

**1** Before the activity, laminate several sheets of the blue paper. Set aside. (If you do not have access to a laminating machine, children can make the clouds directly on a clean tabletop.)

**2** Encourage students to become active cloud watchers. During the course of a week or two, have them draw pictures in their science journals of the clouds they see each day. Students should also note what the weather is like each day. Do different clouds seem to bring different kinds of weather?

**3** Divide the class into small groups. Provide each group with a sheet of laminated paper and a large mound of shaving cream. Have children take turns using the shaving cream to create some of the different cloud shapes they recorded in their journals. What people, animals, or things do the cloud shapes remind other group members of?

**Clouds**
white
gray
thick
puffy
feathery
blowing
drifting
floating
**Clouds**

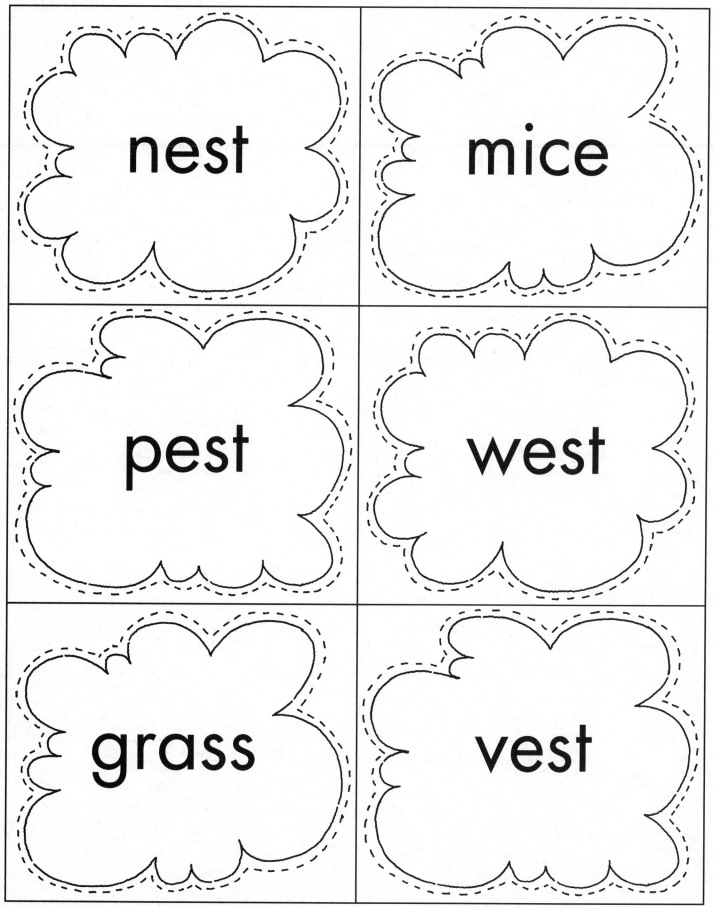

nest

mice

pest

west

grass

vest

best

list

test

face

fish

rest

# Puddle Jumping

The rain came down.
The rain came down,
pitter, pitter, patter.

The time has come.
The time has come,
for splish and splash
and splatter.

Puddle jumping!
Puddle jumping!
Yes, I'm puddle jumping!
My two feet in.
My two feet out.
I feel just like a duckling!

# Puddle Jumping

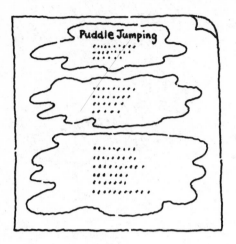

## Introducing the Poem

◎ Write the poem on chart paper. Draw a simple puddle shape around each stanza.

◎ Have children bring their rain boots to school on the day you plan to introduce the poem. As you read the first stanza, children can march in a circle wearing their rain boots. They can turn and march in the other direction as you read the second stanza. And finally, they can stand in place and pretend to jump in and out of puddles as you read the third stanza.

## Talking About the Poem

★ Ask students why we need rain. Help them understand that rain fills our lakes, rivers, and streams; it waters the grass, trees, flowers, and plants we eat; and it gives us water to drink.

★ *Puddle* is such a fun word for children to say. Chant it together several times as you clap out the syllables. Ask children what sounds they hear. Then chant the words *jumping* and *duckling*, again clapping out the syllables. Do students hear a sound that is similar in all three words? (short *u*)

★ Explore with children other fun-sounding words in the poem. Ask, "What words in the poem help you imagine the sound of rain as it falls?" (*pitter, pitter, patter*) Invite children to try saying these words aloud a few times, accentuating their sounds. Explain that words like these sound like their meanings. Ask children if they can find other examples in the poem (*splish, splash, splatter.*)

## Working With Words

**Initial Consonant Jump-Around:** During recess or outside time, use chalk to draw a bunch of puddle shapes on the pavement. Write a word in each shape. Include a number of words that begin with the /p/ sound in *puddle*, as well as words that begin with other consonants. Challenge students to jump from puddle to puddle, landing on only the words that begin with *p*. Lead the rest of the class in chanting the *p* words as children take turns jumping. Repeat the game, focusing on words with the short-*u* sound.

## Shared Writing

**Wet Weather Word Web:**
What do students like to do when the weather is wet and gloomy? Create a word web showing their ideas for rainy day fun.

## Extending the Poem

### Disappearing Puddles

What happens to puddles when the sun comes out? Children can try this simple activity to see for themselves.

**Materials**

- ✳ rain boots
- ✳ copies of the poem "Puddle Jumping" (page 61)
- ✳ chalk

❶ After the next rainfall, take students outside and have a puddle-jumping day. Let children splish and splash as they recite the poem. (If you don't want to wait for a rainy day, you can make your own puddles using a hose. The day before, you may want to send home a note to caregivers asking them to have children bring in or wear footwear that can get wet and muddy.)

❷ When you're through with puddle jumping, have children use the chalk to trace around puddles on hard surfaces. Ask students what they think will happen to the puddles after they sit in the sun for a while.

❸ Check on the puddles one or more times during the course of the day and perhaps the following day. Use the chalk to draw around the puddles each time. What do students notice about the chalk lines? What seems to be happening to the puddles? Ask children what they think is making the puddles shrink. Where do they think the water is going? Review information about the water cycle. (See Talking About the Poem, page 57, and Literature Links, right.)

*Literature Links*

Celebrate the joy of puddle jumping and learn about the water cycle with these books:

*The Puddle* by David McPhail (Farrar, Straus and Giroux, 2000)

*Puddles* by Jonathon London (Puffin, 1999)

*Where Do Puddles Go?* by Allan Fowler (Scholastic, 1995)

# Quiet Seeds

Quiet seeds are sleeping.
They're resting in a row,
patient, precious promises
waiting just to grow.

Quiet seeds are waking.
They're searching for the sun.
Stems and leaves and roots stretch out.
The magic has begun.

Circle-Time Poetry: Science Scholastic Teaching Resources

# Quiet Seeds

## Introducing the Poem

◉ Write the poem on chart paper. Draw the outline of a seed around the words.

◉ Invite students to act out the poem. As you read the first stanza, children can crouch down and pretend to be seeds sleeping in the ground. For the second stanza, they can pretend to wake up and slowly rise toward the sun. Children can spread out their arms to suggest they are growing new leaves.

## Talking About the Poem

✳ Provide children with many different examples of seeds to compare and sort. Tell students that each seed holds the "promise" that new life will grow from it. But seeds can't grow by themselves. Do children know what seeds need to grow? Explain that when seeds receive the right amounts of soil, sun, air, and water, the "magic" begins and seeds grow into plants.

✳ Discuss what it means to be patient. The seeds are patient in the poem because they have to wait for the sun and rain to help them grow. Ask children if they have ever had to sit and wait patiently. Was it difficult? What did they do to stay patient?

✳ Draw students' attention to alliterative phrases such as *resting in a row*; *patient, precious promises*; and *searching for the sun*. What sounds do they hear repeated? What letters make these sounds?

✳ Circle the word *sleeping* in line 1. Can students find the opposite of this word in the poem?

## Working With Words

**Rhyming Word Pocket Chart:** Circle the words *row* and *grow* in the poem. What do students notice about these words? Point out the similar spelling pattern. On an index card, write the word *row*. Write the following initial consonants and consonant clusters on index cards that you have cut in half crosswise: *bl, fl, gl, gr, l, m, s, sh, sl,* and *sn*. Write these letters near the right edge of each card. Place the letters along the bottom of the pocket chart. Ask, "How can we change *row* to *snow*?" Invite a volunteer to place the correct letter card over the *r*. Continue challenging students to form new words by substituting letters.

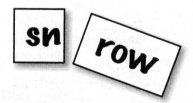

## Literature Links

The following books explore the magic of seeds and the life cycle of plants:

*From Seed to Plant* by Gail Gibbons (Holiday House, 1991)

*How a Seed Grows* by Helene J. Jordan (HarperCollins, 1992)

*The Tiny Seed* by Eric Carle (Simon & Schuster, 1991)

## Shared Writing

**Plant Parts Diagram:** Make a simple drawing of a flowering plant, showing its underground root system. Ask children to help label the parts of the plant: roots, stem, leaves, buds, flowers, petals. Ask children to name the four things a plant needs to grow. Add a sun, soil, and a watering can to the picture, labeling each. Write the word *air* in the space around the plant. Add a row of seeds—waiting patiently underground to grow—and label them as well.

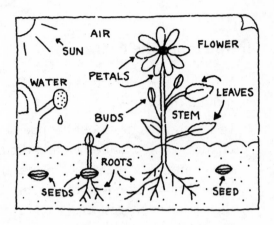

## Extending the Poem

### Funny-Faced Plant Pals

Students can see for themselves what seeds need to grow as they plant grass seeds and watch them sprout.

### Materials

* white paper cups (unwaxed)
* permanent markers
* potting soil
* grass seeds
* watering can
* science journals
* pencils

❶ Provide each child with a paper cup. Have children use markers to draw silly faces on their cups.

❷ Fill each cup with soil, and have children plant the grass seeds. Ask students what the seeds will need to grow.

❸ Have children water the seeds and set the cups on a sunny window ledge. Students should add a little bit of water every day or so to keep the soil moist.

❹ Each day, have children record their observations of the growing process in their journals. As the grass sprouts and grows taller, it will become the "hair" for students' plant pals.

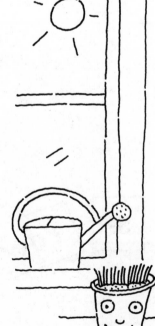

# Hello, Shadow!

Hello, shadow!
Come play with me today.
Let's jump and run and dance.
Come on! I'll lead the way.

Hello, shadow!
We'll have such fun, you'll see!
And when the nighttime comes,
I'll tuck you in with me.

# Hello, Shadow!

## Introducing the Poem

◎ Write the poem on chart paper. Draw a simple picture of a child next to the poem. Use a gray marker to make a shaded area behind the figure that resembles a shadow.

◎ To give your reading a dramatic flair, darken the room and shine a flashlight on a doll or puppet so that its shadow is cast upon the wall. Pretend the doll is talking to its shadow "friend" as you read the poem aloud.

## Talking About the Poem

✴ Begin a discussion about shadows. When and where do students see shadows? Do they see any shadows right now in the room? Can they look out the window and see shadows? Ask students if they know what makes shadows. Explain that a shadow is made when someone or something blocks out the light.

✴ Ask students what sound they hear at the beginning of *shadow*. What letters make this sound? Can they think of other words that begin with /sh/?

✴ Place sticky notes beneath the words *jump, run, such, fun,* and *tuck.* Say each word aloud, then ask students what sound these words have in common.

## Working With Words

**Digraph Shadow Show:** Gather things that begin with *sh,* such as a toy ship, shark, sheep, and shovel; a doll's shirt; a shoe; and a shell. Gather other objects that do not begin with *sh,* such as a key, a watch, a crayon, a pair of scissors, a paper clip, a banana, and a comb. Put the objects in a bag so that students can't see them. One by one, place the objects on an overhead projector. (Tape a file folder onto the light stem of the projector so that students can't see the object.) Ask students to guess the object from its shadow. If the object begins with the /sh/ sound, students should clap. If it doesn't begin with /sh/, they should remain still.

## Shared Writing

**"Dear Shadow" Invitations:** Have children help you write letters inviting their shadows to play. Write the frame below on the chalkboard. Have children think of activities they would like to do with their shadows to complete the frame.

> Dear Shadow,
> Come play with me today.
> We can _____.
>                     Love,
>
>              _____

## Extending the Poem

### Shadow Play Day

Children investigate how their shadows change during the course of a day.

**Materials**
* chalk
* flashlight

1. On the next sunny day, take children outside to play with their shadows early in the morning. Can children make their shadows run, jump, kick, crouch down? Allow time for children to experiment!

2. Divide the class into pairs and have them spread out. Have partners take turns tracing each other's shadow. Partners should also trace each other's footprints to indicate where each child stood to make his or her shadow. Have children write their name on their shadow before heading back to the classroom.

3. In the afternoon, have children return to the outlines of their shadows and stand in the same position they did earlier, using their footprints as a guide. Do their shadows fall in the same place? Why do students think their shadows moved? Help children understand that the sun is in a different position in the sky than it was in the morning. Because the source of light moved, the shadows moved. (Note: Children may think that the sun actually moves in the sky, when in fact it is our planet that is moving around the sun. This concept is probably too abstract for young children to understand. This activity lays the foundation for a deeper understanding of this concept in later years.)

4. Back in class, make the room as dark as possible. Have students take turns using flashlights to cast shadows of their hands on the wall. Challenge children to change the size, shape, and position of their shadow by moving the flashlight. How is this similar to what happened to their shadows on the playground?

**SAFETY NOTE:** Caution children never to look directly at the sun.

# I See the Moon

I see the moon
over houses, grass, and trees.
I see the moon
playing peekaboo with me.

It's peeking through the branches.
It's shining on the lake.
It's cuddling in the clouds now.
Do you think it's still awake?

It's beaming through my window,
on my books and bears and bed.
Now it's smiling at me gently,
"Close your eyes now, sleepy head."

Circle-Time Poetry: Science   Scholastic Teaching Resources

# I See the Moon

## Introducing the Poem

🌀 Write the poem on chart paper. Draw a full moon with a friendly face peering down from the upper corner of the paper. You may want to draw a few stars around the poem as well.

🌀 Children can perform the following actions as you read the poem aloud:

**Lines 1–2**: Pretend to point to moon in sky.
**Lines 3–4**: Play peekaboo.
**Lines 5–6**: Hold arms overhead for branches.
**Lines 7–8**: Cuddle arms around shoulders.
**Lines 9–10**: Trace window shape in air.
**Lines 11–12**: Rest head on hands and pretend to sleep.

## Talking About the Poem

🌟 The moon is often a source of fascination for young children. Invite students to share their observations about the moon. What have they noticed about its shape? Can they describe some of the different shapes they've seen? Have students ever felt as if the moon were watching them or following them? Show students pictures of the different phases of the moon, and introduce them to the names of each phase.

🌟 Ask children to help you orally segment the word *moon*. Can they think of other words that begin with the /m/ sound in *moon*? How about words that have the /o͞o/ sound in the middle? Can they think of other words that end in /n/?

🌟 Point out alliterative phrases such as *cuddling in the clouds* and *books and bears and bed*. What sounds do students hear repeated?

## Working With Words

**"Goodnight, Moon" Phoneme Game:** Draw a "man in the moon" face on a paper plate. Ask children to pretend the plate is the moon and pass it around the circle. As children pass the moon around, recite a list of words that begin with /m/. When children hear you say a word that does not start with /m/, whoever is holding the plate should immediately put it down and say, "Goodnight, moon." Repeat the game, focusing on words with the medial /o͞o/ sound and final /n/ sound.

## Literature Links

Children will delight in the wonder of the moon and its changing appearance as they explore these books:

*Happy Birthday, Moon* by Frank Asch (Simon & Schuster, 2000)

*The Moon Seems to Change* by Franklyn M. Branley (HarperTrophy, 1987)

*Papa, Please Get the Moon for Me* by Eric Carle (Simon & Schuster, 1991)

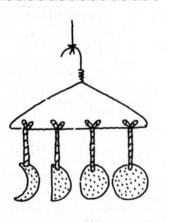

## Shared Writing

**Moon Shape Comparisons:** Ask children if they remember what we call the moon when it is round like a circle. What else can they compare the full moon's round shape to? A coin? An orange? A pizza pie? Write the following sentence frame on the chalkboard five or six times, and ask children to help you complete it:

The full moon is as round as _____.

## Extending the Poem

### Moon Shape Mobiles

Children can make glittering mobiles to illustrate the moon's different phases.

### Materials

* pictures of the moon's phases in books or magazines
* moon phase patterns (page 73)
* heavyweight white paper or card stock
* scissors
* silver glitter
* glue
* hole punch
* yarn
* hangers

❶ Display the pictures of the moon's phases. Review the names of the different phases: *crescent*, *quarter*, *gibbous*, and *full*.

❷ Photocopy page 73 onto heavyweight paper or card stock. Provide each child with a copy of the pattern page. Have students cut out the shapes showing the moon's phases.

❸ Invite children to apply glue to the front and back of each shape and cover with glitter.

❹ Help children punch holes in the shapes. Have them tie one end of a piece of yarn to each shape.

❺ Suspend the shapes from hangers to create mobiles. Use the pictures of the moon phases to guide children in arranging the shapes in the proper order. Display the mobiles around the classroom.

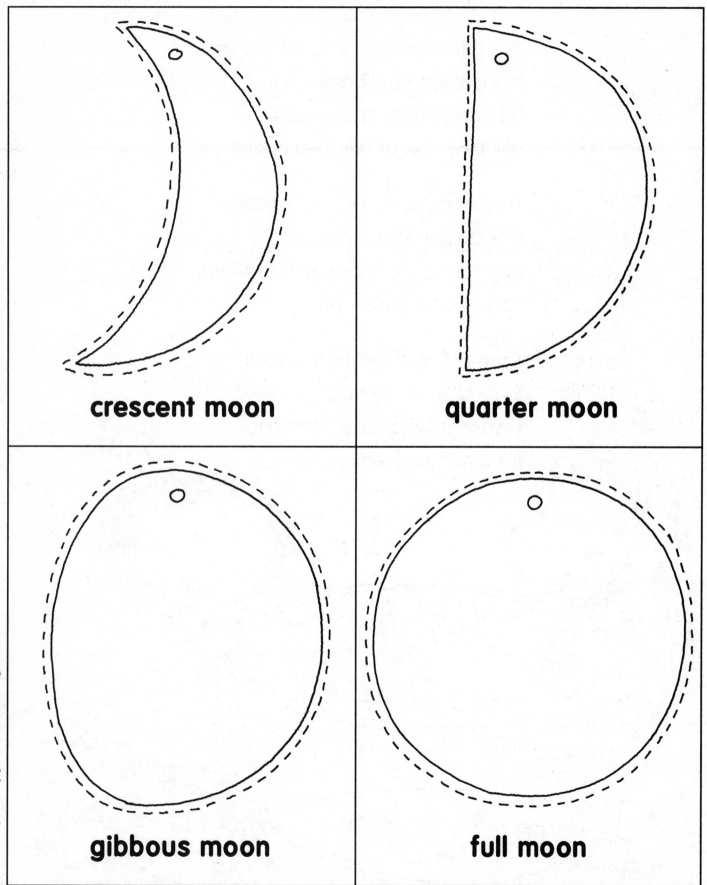

**crescent moon**

**quarter moon**

**gibbous moon**

**full moon**

# Sink or Float?

I've gathered up some treasures
to load upon my boat.
Let's drop them in the water.
Will they sink or will they float?

The marbles, rocks, and pennies
sink quickly. Plop, plop, plop!
But the rubber bands and feathers
float on the water top.

Time to find more treasures
to load upon my boat.
I wonder what else I can find
for a game of sink or float.

9Circle-Time Poetry: Science  Scholastic Teaching Resources

# Sink or Float?

## Introducing the Poem

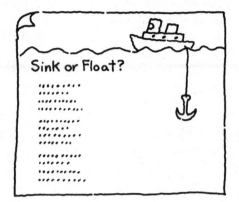

⑨ Near the top of a sheet of chart paper, draw a wavy line to suggest the surface of an ocean or lake. Draw a boat floating on the water's surface and an anchor sinking beneath it. Write the poem beneath the drawing.

⑨ This poem has a strong beat. Invite children to clap their hands or slap their thighs to the rhythm of the words.

## Talking About the Poem

✹ Ask students to think about which things sink or float when they take a bath. Do their rubber ducks sink or float? Does the soap sink or float? How about the washcloth?

✹ Have children help you underline and count the number of times the words *sink* and *float* appear in the poem.

✹ How many words can students find in the poem that are part of the *-op* word family? Invite a volunteer to circle the words.

## Working With Words

**Word Family Action Game:** Children love to say the word *plop*. They'll get plenty of chances to repeat the word in this silly game that focuses on the *-op* word family. Have students stand up in a circle. Move around the circle, asking each child to come up with a word that rhymes with *plop*. Every fourth child should say the word *plop*, then sink down to a sitting position on the floor. Continue playing until all students are seated. Children can use actual words, make up nonsense words, or repeat words, as long as they rhyme with *plop*—for example, *hop, stop, pop, PLOP!; mop, top, zop, PLOP!; slop, flop, dop, PLOP!*

## Shared Writing

**"Sink or Float?" Prediction Chart:** Draw a four-column chart on a chalkboard or sheet of chart paper. Label the columns *Object, My Guess, Does It Sink?,* and *Does It Float?* Have children come up with a list of small objects that they could drop in water to see whether they sink or float. Write these items in the first column. Then ask children to guess whether they think each object will

*(Continues)*

sink or float. Record their guesses in the second column. Test out each object (see Extending the Poem, below), then use check marks in the last two columns to indicate whether the objects sank or floated.

## Extending the Poem

### Sinking Treasures, Floating Treasures

Which objects will sink in a tub of water? Which will float? Students can try this simple experiment to find out.

### Materials

* various small objects (try to test as many objects as possible from your Shared Writing chart; include a balance of objects that will sink—such as keys, pennies, and rocks; and objects that will float—such as feathers, craft sticks, and plastic lids)
* Sink or Float? Chart (page 77)
* pencils
* large, clear plastic container or water table
* water
* clay

❶ Give each child a copy of page 77. Then, before children drop each object into the water, ask them to predict whether the object will sink or float. Have them record their predictions on the chart.

❷ Let children test their predictions, dropping the objects into the water one by one. In separate columns on their chart, have them check off whether each object sank or floated. Were children's guesses correct?

❸ Try one last test. Make several small balls out of the clay. Ask children to predict and record whether the clay balls will float or sink when you drop them in the water. Drop the clay balls in and watch them sink. Then challenge students to try to mold the clay balls into other shapes that they can make float. Test out their ideas.

# Sink or Float?

| Object | My Guess | Does It Sink? | Does It Float? |
|--------|----------|---------------|----------------|
|        |          |               |                |
|        |          |               |                |
|        |          |               |                |
|        |          |               |                |
|        |          |               |                |

# Do You Know Sounds?

Do you know sounds?
Quiet sounds, quiet sounds,
these are quiet sounds:
lullabies
a breeze that sighs
a fly that's buzzing near
a mouse's squeak
tiptoes that sneak
a whisper in my ear.

Do you know sounds?
LOUD SOUNDS, LOUD SOUNDS
these are BIG, LOUD SOUNDS:
stomping feet
horns that beep
a barking dog outside
a lion's roar
a slamming door
a roller-coaster ride.

Circle-Time Poetry: Science  Scholastic Teaching Resources

# Do You Know Sounds?

## Introducing the Poem

◎ Write the poem on the left side of a sheet of chart paper. Draw a large, simple diagram of an ear on the right side of the poem.

◎ Use a whispery voice as you read about the quiet sounds in the first stanza of the poem. Use a booming voice as you read about the loud sounds in the second stanza of the poem.

## Talking About the Poem

✴ Tell children that sounds are made by vibrations—very quick back-and-forth movements that are made over and over again. Place your hand over your throat and invite children to do the same, then reread the poem together. Ask children to describe what they feel. Tell them this sensation is their vocal cords vibrating, or moving, to create sounds.

✴ Invite children to make some of the sounds in the poem. Can they buzz quietly like a fly? Squeak like a mouse? Tiptoe around the room? Can they stomp their feet noisily? Beep like a car horn? Roar like a lion?

✴ Use sticky notes to cover all but the initial consonant or consonant cluster of several words in the poem. For example, cover all but the *fl* in *fly*, the *m* in *mouse*, and the *wh* in *whisper*. Can students guess each missing word based on its beginning sound?

## Working With Words

**Opposites Match-Up:** Point out that the words *quiet* and *loud* are opposites. Ask students to think of other pairs of opposites (for example, *wet/dry, in/out, up/down, good/bad, fat/thin,* and *happy/sad*). Write each word on a separate index card. Punch holes in the upper corners of each card and tie a length of yarn through the holes. Give each child a word card necklace to wear around his or her neck. Challenge each student to find the classmate wearing the word card that is the opposite of the word on his or her own card.

## Literature Links

For more information about how sounds are produced, as well as some noisy fun, share these books with students:

*Achoo! Bang! Crash! The Noisy Alphabet* by Ross MacDonald (Roaring Brook, 2003)

*The Science Book of Sound* by Neil Ardley (Harcourt, 1991)

*Sounds All Around* by Wendy Pfeffer (HarperTrophy, 1999)

## Shared Writing

**Noisy/Quiet Word Webs:** Have students come up with as many noisy and quiet sounds as they can. Create two word webs showing their ideas.

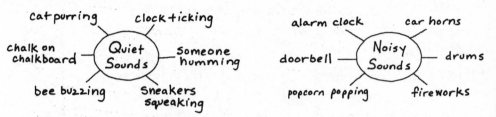

## Extending the Poem

### Noisy Sound Shakers

Students can experiment with sound by making these simple rhythm instruments.

**Materials**
- heavyweight paper plates
- art materials (crayons, paints, markers, glitter, sequins, and so on)
- dried beans or popcorn
- glue

1 Provide each child with two paper plates. Tell children to decorate the back of both plates using the art materials.

2 Have children place one of their plates faceup on their desk. Put a handful of dried beans or popcorn on each child's plate.

3 Show students how to spread glue around the rim of the plate with the beans or popcorn on it. They should then turn the other plate upside down and place it on top of the first plate, pressing along the rims to glue the plates together.

4 Invite children to shake their plates as they march around the room. How quiet can they make their shakers sound? How loud can they make them sound?